Living and Succeeding with Schizophrenia

By: John Witcher

This book is dedicated to Allen Brown

In 1994, I was diagnosed with schizophrenia. This disease changed my life and had a lasting effect on my family. In this book, I will share my story and I will talk about the things that helped me reach my goals. Every person is different, but the obstacles that I have faced have given me the tools that I need to help individuals and families that face mental illnesses. There are many organizations that can be helpful when a person is in need of assistance. At the end of this book, I have listed the websites of companies and organizations that can be very helpful in times of need.

It is very hard to explain the fear and anxiety that a person feels when they face a mental illness. When I started to face the problems that schizophrenia thrust upon me, I needed emotional guidance and answer that no one had. If you or a loved one has experienced this disease, you know how physically and mentally draining that it can be on the patient and the family. It is very important to remember that you cannot face these types of problems alone. The healing process can be slow and it is important to remember that there is help. I can remember that it felt like my world had shattered. The initial mental shut down was draining and then anger. Why did this have to happen to me? It is important to remember that you will not have all the answers. Even if it seems that your loved one is not making progress, trust me, they are glad to have you near. In the early stages, it is important to let your loved one know that it will get better. I can remember my mother saying, "I promise, it will get better." The early stages of my mental illness were a blur, but as I started responding to treatment, I got strength from those types of words.

I want to begin our journey with the early stages of my recovery. The first step to my recovery started with a neat program. The program was called Pathways and it was introduced in an extraordinary fashion. Please keep in mind that the depression and denial that ensue after facing schizophrenia can be incredibly hard to handle. After being released from the hospital, I moved into a group home. It was a little strange living with individuals that I had never met. For the first two weeks, I sat in my room and listened to music. I thought to myself over and over again, why me? In a few weeks, I learned that most of the people living with me were facing the same problems that I was. In a matter of months, I was becoming very self-sufficient. This is where the Pathways program came into play. Now that I did not feel so alienated, I joined the program. It is a great program and I made big strides in a short time. I would get up one morning a week and work in the snack bar. One day I was at the register and another day I was behind the counter. The next week, I was in the computer lab learning basic computer skills. It was a great sense of accomplishment. After a few weeks, I started going to the program two days a week. This is a big step for a person with schizophrenia. It is hard to explain the fear of new people and public places that were strong in the early years. The staff was very sensitive to the feelings that I had and made me feel very comfortable. It is very important to listen to your loved ones feelings. When I felt comfortable and knew I could be honest, it was like something had changed. I grew into a person that liked to face challenges. I encourage you to get your loved ones into these types of programs. Your local mental health organizations can do things that your family does not have the resources to do. I was never told that I should not attempt to accomplish a goal because people with schizophrenia cannot do these things. I was told that if I start to do things on my own, I can do anything that I want to accomplish.

After four months in pathways, I took a big step. I got a job and began to work in the evenings. The work was tedious, but it gave me a sense of accomplishment. I had been living on welfare and it felt good to make a step on my own. As I got more serious about my job, they cut my welfare little by little. I started paying one bill. After a while, I picked up a couple of other bills. Before I knew it, I was self-sufficient. I was taking care of myself, for the first time in my life. It was a good feeling to know that my doctor and case- managers were there if I needed them, but I had a sense of accomplishment that I had never had. I started to write short stories and read novels. I was doing better than I had ever done. There were three years that I grew like I could not believe. Then I did something that almost took it all away. I began to drink on the weekends. Then I began to drink after work. Then I began to drink every day. After all that I had accomplished, I was admitted back into the hospital. It is very easy to stumble. I did not let this stop me. This problem just slowed me down. In a couple of months I was sober and I have been sober for 13 years. I am sure my family was crushed by my relapse, but please remember that your loved one is not perfect. On a warm summer night, I did something that I had always dreamed about, I enrolled in college. My grades in high school were not that great, so I got into school on academic probation. I studied like I never had. I failed the English placement test and the math placement test. Having done this, I started at the bottom. I worked in my text books for hours every night. I got grants and student loans and slowly made my way through classes. I made A's in my classes and was soon off academic probation. I have always wished that the government would set aside grants for people with mental illnesses. Having gone through the system, I know how hard it is to get funds for school. With an education, a person with a mental illness has more options. There is a great program called the Lilly Reintegration Scholarship. The drug giant, Eli Lilly, offer this scholarship to people with mental illnesses that are working to get an education. I am grateful to Lilly for offering this program, and I wish that more companies would take steps to make such a big difference to those that could not achieve their education goals without such assistance.   Thanks to companies like this and countless individuals, I receive an associate of science and a bachelor of science. In the beginning goals like these can be a little overwhelming. It is important to take it one step at a time. When I started going to Pathways, I could have never guessed that I would be able to live the life that I had always wished for. Once a patient has improved enough to function in a work environment, there is a program called Supported Employment. This program focuses on the patient's strengths and helps find suitable employment. I have also listed the information on Vocational Rehabilitation and Supported Employment at the end of this book. There are many things that are vital to recovery, but the one thing that I found to be a key factor in recovery is self-esteem. There are several ways to build self-esteem, but I think that setting goals works the best. As I got on the road to recovery, I began to set reasonable goals. When setting goals, I think that it is imperative to set three types of goals.

It helps to set three short term goals that can be achieved in one year, three mid-range goals that can be achieved in five years, and three long-term goals that can be achieved in ten years. When setting goals it helps to remember that they do not have to be earth shattering or amazing feats. I just set goals that I had always wanted to achieve. You will be amazed at the self-esteem that will be built when you achieve even one of your short-term goals. Then there are those long-term goals that you must work really hard to achieve. The nice thing about the long-term goals is that they keep you working very hard, and once you have achieved a short-term goal, you know that you can reach those long-term goals. I also found that having comforting relationships builds self-esteem. Friends tend to bring out the best in each other. When you find someone that cares about you and your dreams, you grow indefinitely. Even with self-esteem, you are going to have low points that occur in your life. The nice thing about building self-esteem through relationships is that you learn how to communicate much more effectively. It might sound strange, but communication was the thing that I struggled with in most of my relationships. Schizophrenia can make communicating even more difficult than one could ever imagine. As I said, I always feared the way that people perceived or judged me because of the fact that I have a mental illness. This destroyed my chances of building self-esteem for many years. It is hard for a person with a mental illness to make a first move in a relationship, especially in the early stages. I found that I was a rewarding individual to be around, but I made very destructive choices. Choices can affect self-esteem as much as any other factor. I had always taken for granted that everyone that I met and shared a relationship with would help me grow. The truth is that no matter how much you try, some people will take advantage of kindness. I went through a relationship that was unimaginably difficult, I felt so low that it took months to recover. As a parent, I think that you should step into a person's life and help them avoid destructive choices. I am not saying that you should try to take total control of your loved one's life, but show support. It is good for your loved one to do things on their own, but they will need guidance.   At the age that my schizophrenia set in, I had almost no life skills. I struggled with this for years and years. Marrying my wife was one of the most rational choices that I ever made. My wife cares about herself and she also cares about me. In destructive relationships, I found that some people do not love themselves. Like the proverb says, if you do not love yourself, you cannot love someone else. It is great for self-esteem to learn to love yourself. I spent so many years doing things that I thought that my friends would like that I never experienced life for myself. I had no idea how to love myself. I think I feared this thought for many years. It may be why it was so painful to be alone.

If your loved one seems to be struggling with self-esteem, try to encourage the individual to set one goal. I can tell you that it will not be easy. This is true, especially in the early stages of a mental illness. It is very easy to get the feeling that you are worthless and that everything you do is worthless. If your loved one wants to have some poetry published, encourage them to write poetry. This is one technique that I used to build goals as I moved forward through my mental illness. I set a goal to start writing poetry and then one of the staff of the group home told me about a writing contest and I entered it. It was the first thing that I had ever had published and it put a spark of energy back in my life. Believe me, the first goal that a person achieves will make a huge difference in their outlook on life. I went from believing that I could not do anything, to believing that I could accomplish something. If you or your loved one has a hard time setting goals, try to set goals by incorporating hobbies. There are literally millions of hobbies that are fun and reasonably inexpensive. If your loved one has a passion for writing, they can by a notebook and keep a journal. It is healthy to be able to look back on the struggles and achievements that have happened in a person's life.

Several of my classes required that I kept a journal to see how my thoughts on certain subjects changed after I learned a great deal more about them. I have friends that started sewing on a daily basis. After a couple of years the items that were created were amazing. After creating some very nice items, she was able to sell her items on consignment in a craft shop. Not only did she reach her goal of being able to market her creations, but other people got to enjoy something that she created. In the beginning, it may take a while to see that goals are going to bring change, but I guarantee they are worth every minute of work. There are countless ways to build self-esteem. I think that exercise is great for building self-esteem. There are many complications that can arise from lack of exercise. Exercise not only builds self-esteem, it also helps maintain it. A great deal of mental health facilities have an exercise room on their grounds. If the mental health facility that you or a loved is a part of does not have an exercise room, it would not hurt to recommend it. If there is not an exercise area that is available, start to take walks with your loved one. Walking is great exercise and it is a great way to get them to open up to you. Taking walks is also a great way to get into a routine. You can start taking walks one time a week for about twenty minutes and gradually build on minutes and days. I promise you that you will not regret getting into this type of routine. If your loved one has access to a work out facility, this is also a great way to make friends. When two friends get into a routine, it is amazing the positive things that can happen. I also think that employment is a very good way to build self-esteem. The problem that most people with mental illnesses face is healthcare. Since medication and care are so expensive, it is very difficult for most people with mental illnesses to work. I think that even if a person with a mental illness works part time, it will boost self-esteem. It feels great to function on your own, especially with the challenges that those with schizophrenia face. When I was a teenage boy and I was living with my parents, I never worked. I guess, even as I got older, that I expected to get whatever I wanted. I thought that I was happy living in this manner. When I got out on my own and started working and buying the things that I wanted, my self-esteem grew immensely. It is scary trying to build an independent life, and it causes stress on the patient and the family. The one thing that I recommend in recover, it is moderation. I think that moderation is important from the onset of a mental illness and even after years of recovery. The reason that I think that moderation is so important is very simple. It is easy to work on more aspects of recover with moderation. If a patient dives wholeheartedly into working, it can cause problems with other aspects of recovery. When I was in the early stages of recovery, I would try to juggle a few different tasks. If a patient works in moderation, when serious stress hits it is easier to cope with the problems. Even when a person is independent, make sure that they are not afraid to ask for help. I was very fearful of working and being independent. In the beginning there were so many questions going through my mind. What if I need help? Will I be expected to take care of all of the issues that arise in my life? This was not the case at all. Remember, at the age that a male faces schizophrenia, they have not had the chance to build all the necessary life skills. This brings me to another point that I would like to make. I picked up a great deal of important life skills from working. At work you must interact and function with others. This is hard for those that do not have mental illnesses, so you can imagine the added stress that a mental illness adds. I do think that the benefits of working are higher than the drawbacks.   There is nothing in the world like friendship. Making friends can be an incredible way to build self-esteem. When you have someone outside your immediate family that you know that you can count on and they know that they can count on you, things change. It is not easy to build friendship, especially with schizophrenia. When I tell a person that I have schizophrenia, there opinion of me changes almost immediately. This deflated my self-esteem for so many years. I think that my attitude was as much to blame as those that were around me. I think that it might sound strange, but I always thought that I needed to prove that I could accomplish just as much as those without a mental illness. I learned that friends will love you no matter what your level of success is. I realize that you must earn respect, but you must also build friendship. When a friend learns that they can trust and rely on you, a very important strength is formed. I never really thought much about building friendship until I had a conversation with a friend that has schizophrenia. He said that he would love to have someone that he could talk to that he thought would not judge him from what he had to say to them. I listened to what he said and from that point on, I tried to listen without any discrimination toward him. After I would talk to him, he would stay on my mind for days. He is a very bright individual, but he has very low self-esteem. I can tell you from experience that self-esteem will change an attitude like most cannot believe. Never underestimate the power that a friend's love can have on self-esteem.

Doing things on my own helped me build self-esteem, especially in the early stages of the illness. Since men develop schizophrenia in the late teen years, most that I have met did not develop common life skills. It may be tough on the family member to let a patient grow while they are really struggling, but as long as your loved one is not headed for a terrible decision, it is good to let them grow. When I lived in the group home, I learned to take care of myself. What most considered common life skills, I struggled with. Learning to take care of myself was a frightening process, but it made me strong and I am grateful for those that made me take those steps. Your loved one needs your support, but they also need to grow. Give them some boundaries and make them take steps toward personal independence. I promise you, someday they will thank you. I know that it is a frightening thought for you and your loved one, but someday you are not going to be there to take care of them. If the thought of them struggling to learn how to take care of themselves scares you, image if you were not there at all. My family has always been there for me to lean on, but since I gained some independence, they have really let me grow. It is a proud feeling to know that I am independent. I worry sometimes. Everyone in life worries at one time or another. But learning to live makes all those trouble worthwhile. It is like studying for a final exam. I would worry and almost be a basket case, but when it was over the feelings that followed were amazing.

I would like to discuss a subject that I feel very strong about. That subject is substance abuse. I am not sure if it is a coincidence or not, but most of the people that I have met with mental illnesses have suffered from substance abuse at one time or another. I learned at a support group many years ago that substance abuse can mask the symptoms of mental illnesses such as schizophrenia. I got into drug abuse as a teen and it nearly wrecked my life. I have heard that drug abuse that occurs in teenage years while a certain part of the brain is developing may be linked to mental illnesses. If you even suspect that your teen is abusing drugs, it is very important to get involved. There are organizations that can help a parent combat substance abuse. I have listed information about an organization called DARE at the end of this book. DARE can help parents combat drug abuse. The abuse of prescription drugs has become alarming. Your loved one does not need a drug dealer to get drugs, they just need to go to the medicine cabinet. I hope that the link between drug abuse and mental illnesses is indeed true. If this is the case, there is a sure fire way to combat diseases such as schizophrenia. It may be hard for a parent to accept, but if your loved one does not want you to know that they are abusing drugs, you probably will drugs has become alarming. Your loved one does not need a drug dealer to get drugs, they just need to go to the medicine cabinet. I hope that the link between drug abuse and mental illnesses is indeed true. If this is the case, there is a sure fire way to combat diseases such as schizophrenia. It may be hard for a parent to accept, but if your loved one does not want you to know that they are abusing drugs, you not know. My mother had no idea that I was abusing drugs until it was too late. If your loved one is an adult you can still make a difference by intervening. I can tell you from experience that your loved one is not going to say that they have a problem. I would always tell my friends that I could give up drugs whenever I wanted. So one day a friend mine said, "Prove it." I was caught off guard by this blunt approach, but I made an effort. In times of relapse and in the midst of hardcore substance abuse, friendship can be a beacon of light. Something else that I learned is that friends can shape a person. If your friends are into hardcore substance abuse, the odds are you will be into it too. I tried to stop taking drugs several times, but I felt like an outcast. All my friends were doing it, so I looked like an odd ball. Then I got involved with friends that had goals and families and they were respected. I started going to their family functions and holiday parties and found that I could have fun without abusing drugs. It is a difficult process to change something that has been a part of life for so many years. Humans are creatures of habit. I sometimes wonder if I had not been so into drugs when I was in high school, if I would have made some of the terrible mistakes that I made. I started substance abuse when I was very young. I can remember that a friend of mine would clean out cologne bottles really well and we would fill them with liquor. We would carry them around and no one had any idea that they had liquor in them. I abused drugs several times a week with that individual and this brings me back to a point that I made earlier. This individual has suffered from mental problems as well. That is why it is so important to intervene into the life of a loved one to get them on the right path. Again, I tell you from experience that you will have harsh words when you are trying to get a loved one on the right path, but someday they will thank you for it.   It is also good to call and become acquainted with the parents of your children's friends. When I was a child, I did drugs with some of my friends parents. It is so important for some parents to seem cool that they think that this is acceptable. When it comes to substance abuse, expect the unexpected.

There are things that make a difference in life that do not seem significant. I think that at the end of each day a person should reflect on the day's events. Some write down the day's events in a journal, I find comfort in a twenty minute reflection. It is good to look at the day and think of what you can do tomorrow to make yourself a little happier. It is not healthy to dwell on bad thoughts, but I am sure that there are a least a couple of items of joy that a person experiences over the course of the day. I have also found that a comforting nightly reflection makes me sleep a little more sound. If you do not reflect on events that were significant over the day, sometimes the mind begins to race. I sometimes have terrible nightmares and I really used to struggle with this issue. With a nightly reflection, I have found that if I focus on comforting thoughts that happened throughout the day, I have fewer nightmares. Reflection can also be comforting in the early stages of schizophrenia. If a patient is in a hospital or group home, a comfortable nightly reflection can help ease the anxiety of being away from home. I have learned to never underestimate the power of positive thoughts. The people that I met that were always negative recovered at a much slower rate. I really encourage that positive reflection is practiced.

Moral support kept me going, even through some very hard times. Support is very important to the patient and family. Whether it was my mom sitting with me in the hospital or may dad playing basketball with me at that group home, moral support is priceless. When you develop a disease like schizophrenia, you find out who you true friends are. Your loved one may seem angry or closed off. This is not anybody's fault. It is easy to blame yourself. You cannot believe the feelings that are experienced by a person that has a mental illness. On top of this, we are facing drug side effects. Some patients are on more than one medication. Please take this into account when they seem a little troubled. Some of my friends in the group home said that they do not tell the mental health staff anything. This can set recovery back a long way. I know that I felt better talking to my family and letting them discuss problem with the mental health staff, especially when I had just met a staff member.

Peers can change the life of a person with a mental illness. It is very important to surround yourself with positive people. It will be hard to convince your loved one that they are surrounding themselves with the wrong friends. If your loved one is trying to stop smoking cigarettes, it is not a good idea to hang around with smokers. If your loved one is trying to stop drinking, it is not a good idea to be in relationships with people that are consumed with these types of problems. I tried several times to quit smoking cigarettes. When I started to make friends that did not smoke cigarettes, it made the process so much easier. I think that a person is a reflection of their friends. Attitude can change a person's life. By keeping a good attitude, a person can make a terrible situation into a growing experience. It is hard to stay positive when everyone that you communicate with seems negative. If you talk about the positive things in your life and the positive things in your loved one's life, it will make a lasting difference. My mom has a way of finding the silver lining in any situation. That is one of the reason that I like to spend time with her. From the day that I was diagnosed with schizophrenia, my mother has been a strong positive influence in my personal growth. It is hard to comprehend what a positive visit with a loved one can do. When I was hospitalized, those positive visits from mom were the only thing that kept me going. I am sure it was hard for her to stay positive, but she did. When I was in the group home, the positive visits from my dad were sometimes the only thing that got me out of bed. It may sound strange, but with schizophrenia, relationships were very hard to maintain. With schizophrenia, trust can be very difficult. This is very true, especially in the early stages of the illness. I spent a great deal of time trying to find someone that could relate to me. With the way people perceive you when they find out you have a mental illness, it seems that I was always looking for some sort of approval. Most people with mental illnesses do not get a chance to be around groups of people. I can remember that dating scared me to death. The thing that makes relationship even tougher is prejudice. Everyone knows that if an individual from a certain race commits a terrible crime, it seems that people blame the race and not the individual. I think that this holds true for mental illnesses as well. Someone does something terrible and pleads insanity and there goes any hope of being trusted. I think that it is important for individuals with mental illnesses to have relationships that create trust. My wife changed the way I think about everything. It was a chance encounter that turned out to be extraordinary. My wife is loving, trustworthy, kind, and patient. With the stages of growth that a person faces when they are coping with a mental illness, it can make it very tough to know when that person is ready for a relationship. It is very important to remember that trust is a very difficult matter for those with schizophrenia. It took me thirty-six years to trust a person enough to get married. With my new found relationship, there were signs of growth. I began to reach for my dreams and started to achieve them at a fast rate. I served as a grant panelist in the Indiana Arts Commission. I got my bachelor's degree and I even got a black belt in Tae Kwon Do. My wife and my family have given me countless gifts with the word dream on them. This may sound strange, but I think that setting and achieving goals causes emotional growth. It really upsets me when I hear an individual talk down about the sanity of an individual because they have a relatively outlandish dream. This is where family is vital. I believe that society is not going to change any time soon, and this can be emotionally crushing. It is really hard to comprehend the stress that a mental illness can put on a family. I remember that I did not think that I had a problem. In the early stages it is important to find help with the situation, as it can get out of control fast. It is overwhelming to try and take on this hardship alone. When you start to see symptoms, it is important to take action. Males usually develop schizophrenia at a younger age than females. I can tell you from experience, the person that is facing the mental illness is confused, angry, and completely lost. When you approach the person, they may say things that really are not like the person that you know and love. I can tell you that years down the road they will thank you for helping them with such a big burden. It is obvious that a mental illness is hard on the patient, but it is also hard on the family. Most families do not know what to do in this type of situation, so it can be a terrible experience. I think that it is comforting for family members to talk to other mothers, fathers, or sibling that have a person in the immediate family that has a mental illness. They can offer advice and show general concern, this is comforting.

Once the family and patient have made it through the initial phase of the illness, the healing begins. I spent years in therapy and I think that it really helped. It is a good idea to talk to the patient's therapist. It is also important to tell the patient (they will be more apt to listen to a family member in the early stages) to be honest with their therapist. The therapist cannot help if the patient is not open and honest with them. It is a little rough in the early stages of the mental illness. I sometimes felt threatened by the questions that my therapist was asking me. What I did not understand was that he needed to know what kind of issues I was having if he was going to be able to make my treatment work. I can remember sitting silent with a blank stare as my therapist tried to get me to open up. After a couple of sessions, I found that we had some things in common. You cannot expect miracles in the early stages of schizophrenia, and trust is a real issue for patients when they are learning to cope with a mental illness. One thing that can made therapy hard in the early stages was being afraid that I was going to give a wrong answer. It is important that you or your loved one learn to be open. There are no right or wrong answers, it is just what can we do to make the healing process begin.

After my first week in the group home, I found that most of the people that I spoke with in the group home were afraid of change. Because of the age that schizophrenia takes a hold of a person's life and the implications that will follow, you must be ready for some serious changes. This is true for families and patients. It seemed that I went through some sort of change every year. Those changes caused me to grow and become a person that learned to live for challenges. With my substance abuse and my unwillingness to try to achieve anything in my teenage years, I was not prepared for reality. This is something that you may want to focus on, because when a mental illness hits, you are going to get a hard dose of reality. As terrible as this sounds, there is comfort in surviving in the real world. As much as a parent wants to be there for their children, it is important to remember that someday you are not going to be there. If you feel terrible watching them struggle and learn hard truths, you should feel a little comfort knowing that they are learning to be self-sufficient. Most people will not care as much as a parent does, so let them take steps on their own. I remember how hard it was on my mom to watch me adapt to my changing life, but now she smiles every time I make an accomplishment. When I was in the group home I saw both parents and patients break down. I promise that the changes that take place in the early stages of schizophrenia are the hardest to handle. It just gets better and better in a gradual manner. I can remember the look on my mom's face when I got on the school bus for the first time. She had the same look during the first month of my hospitalization. I think that I tend to make her smile a great deal more these days. After all we have been through, those smiles are worth more than any amount of money.

Something that took me a while to learn is that a person will occasionally fail. It is human to fail. It is impossible to succeed at everything. The main thing to remember is that you should learn from your failures. Coping with failure can be very tough, but it builds character. A friend of mine once told me that you only fail when you stop trying. There were times when I wanted to give up. I wanted to just throw my hands in the air. This is where my family and friends gave me strength. My mom said to me, "remember what it took you to get where you are now." I reflect on those words every day. I have found that it is not healthy to dwell on the past, but it is very healthy to remember what it took to get you where you are. I have faced some serious hardships working to take care of myself, but they do not compare to those first four weeks of my mental illness. This is the type of thing that you should have your loved one focus on, especially if they are dealing with some sort of failure.

I have also found that it is very important to find your strengths. When you are struggling with a mental illness it is not easy to find your strengths. If you do not use your strengths, you may as well not have them. I have met quite a few people with mental illnesses and they seem to think that accomplishments are out of reach. I talked about using strengths quite a bit during my reflection on goals, but I cannot emphasize this enough. You will honestly be amazed at the results of finding and using strengths. When finding strengths, it is also important to find weaknesses. When you find weaknesses, you can make leaps toward recovery. To help with recovery, it is important to get help with things you do not do well. There is not a person alive that can do everything well. I do my best to use my strengths and get help with the things that I do not do well. The biggest problem that I had was admitting that I was having trouble with something. In business classes we would do a SWOT Analysis on a company or organization. SWOT stands for strengths, weaknesses, opportunities, and threats. I think that a person can apply this concept to their life. Once a person has a list of their strengths and weaknesses, they can focus on their opportunities. It will be amazing to you and your loved one on just how many opportunities that there are for them. I usually approach threats in a different manner. It is important to know that a problem may arise in the recovery process, so it is important to list them. I really think that the majority of the focus should be on the positive aspects of recovery.

I want to take some time to focus on the onset of a mental illness. In the beginning, it is important to take it one day at a time. If I could make one suggestion that will make a world of difference, it is positive reinforcement. I found so much comfort in things that were so simple to create. You will be amazed at how your loved one will react to photos that they like. My mom makes these little photo collages. When I was in a very troubles state of mind, I found comfort in these photos. It was a soothing feeling to see those happy moments that seemed so far away. Music was also soothing. Music can have an effect on emotions that is hard to explain. I would listen to positive music and it seemed that my mood would change immediately. The problem that you will probably have in the very early stages of the illness is that your loved one is not going to tell you what brings them comfort. Most parents have a pretty good idea of what make their children happy. One thing that concerns me is that the parents also need something that brings them comfort. This is where the mental health organizations are priceless. You can bet that there are support groups with individuals that have been right where you are and I am sure that they will be glad to help. Do not be afraid to ask for help. Your loved one will need you to be strong and focused on their recovery. My mom got a great deal of strength from my grandmother. There are people that will be there for you so that you can be there for your loved one. Some of the parents I came in contact with seemed afraid to ask for help. The biggest gift that you will be able to give is love. Love has an effect on people like nothing else does. I can remember thinking, especially as I started to recover, wow I cannot believe how much my parents, doctors, and case workers actually care about me. I was not a case number, I was someone that they wanted to see living a good life. I had no idea that taking steps on my own would feel so good. There are things in my life that are very hard, but they lead to the things that take my breath away. One other thing that I found to be comforting in the hospital, group home, and on my own is decorating for the holidays. There is something about decorations during holiday seasons that bring a feeling of happiness. In the group home we always decorated, and my mom was kind enough to give me this little Christmas tree that I put in my room. I think it is important to keep something cheerful in every room. This is great to do because you see these decoration before you go to bed and when you get up in the morning. In the early stages of my illness, when I saw a decoration, it brought back comforting memories of great family times.

One of the problems that I faced that was incredibly hard to deal with was loneliness. In the early months of living in the group home and even when I first moved into an apartment, I was terribly lonely. I felt awkward about calling my friends because I did not know how they would react to my mental illness. I did not work, so I watched television until I could not stand it anymore. I chain smoked. For some reason it seemed to keep me somewhat content. I felt kind of alienated, so I did not read, play my guitar, or write. I was also concerned that getting back in with my friends would bring even more bad habits. Then a friend of mine called and said he wanted to get together and play some music. He does not drink or smoke, so I told him that I would like to make some music together. This was like an incredible form of therapy for me. These guys are incredible musicians and it was so much fun. Mark lived right across the street from the campus, so people would wander in and out. This helped me build some confidence and make some friends. We played music at his house for a few weeks and then we started performing at university functions. The university's staff was sincerely nice, and this made for lasting relationships. I talked earlier about getting a college degree and the people that I met when we performed at these functions helped make that possible. The compassion that I got when I was in need is one of the things that drives me to help people that want to achieve and function, especially those with mental illnesses. It would be a lie to say that I was not scared to death the first day that I sat in class at the university. I think that being alone actually help my grades. Instead of sitting around smoking cigarettes and trying to occupy my long and empty days, I studied. I studied like I never had. I did more than the homework that was assigned. I read chapters until I thoroughly understood them. In two years I became a member of the Alpha Sigma Lambda National Honor Society. The point that I am trying to make is when your loved one seemed to be alone or struggling to occupy their time, encourage them to make a positive focus. I will admit that school is not for everyone, but there are positive program that anyone can try that will occupy their time and help take steps forward. I recommend some form of program that encourages communication. My lack of communication skills brought me trouble for years. Fear was the one thing that made it hard for me to communicate. I would always think to myself, what if they think that what I say sounds stupid. I felt inferior for most of my life. I think that my feeling came from so much isolation. I got used to be alone. It is easy for someone with a mental illness to use their illness to justify isolation. When I got into a healthy relationship, I was dumbfounded. I could not believe that I had been missing out on this type of companionship. I had been in so many terrible relationships as a teen that isolation brought comfort. Then I met the woman that I married. Outside of my mom, my sister, my grandma, and my Aunt Brenda I really did not have females that I knew, loved, and trusted. It was a strange feeling in the early months of my marriage. The relationship that I have with my wife is therapeutic. It is amazing how much a work day changes when I think about my wife or hear from my wife. After having my heart broken by my high school sweetheart, I had been afraid to think about having a relationship like that. When you have a mental illness, you do not always get a chance at love that is undying. I lived in the darkness for so many years. I waited and waited for someone to turn on the light. I did not realize that I could do it myself. When that light comes on in a part of your life, there is a chain reaction.

Another problem that I faced in the early stages of my mental illness was the harsh reality. I had plenty of time to think about my problems. The mental health organization that I was a part of did something really fun.

They organized a softball league for those with mental illnesses. This was amazingly fun. I had been cooped up all winter and really needed something like this. We were in the park, so you can imagine how great it felt. It was a sunny day with a light breeze. The exercise brought the fresh air into my lungs and it was sweet. I saw my friends that had mental illnesses smile like I had never seen them smile. When you talk to the people that can make a difference, I encourage you to recommend these types of activities. I also saw this when I was in the group home. There is a basketball goal in the parking lot. I mentioned that I think that exercise is imperative to physical and mental health, but in the early spring it is different. After a long winter, that first breath of spring air can change even the worst attitude. I spoke earlier in the book about taking walks. My wife and I take walks together and we seem to open up on these walks. Never underestimate the healing power of a soothing breeze. The nice thing about taking advantage of a nice day is that you can reflect on it all week. A friend of mine told me that a little sunshine goes a long way. I think that this is true. And you do not have to pay a bunch of money to enjoy a nice afternoon. It gives you an excuse to go out and have fun.

It may take some time for a patient to open up to their therapist, but it is very healthy for a patient to be honest with their therapist. However, I think that it is important to have someone that you can share your thoughts with outside a clinical setting. I had so many days that were filled with emptiness. Then one day it happened. I was working in the snack bar in Pathways and I met a kind person. He was much older than me, but he was kind and soft spoken. He started talking to me and I enjoyed his conversation. He was being treated for depression and said that his days were long. I could sure relate to that, as I have had some long days myself. I think in the early days of Pathways, it was his company that made me interested in going. He would talk about how things have changed and what he thought about it. He did not really complain much, but he had his own opinions. Having known this person taught me that you can make a difference in someone's life without worrying what they will think about you. I sometimes think that if I had not met this person, I may have not recovered as fast. That is another thing that makes programs that mental health organizations offer so effective. I can assure you that your loved one will relate to people that are facing the same problems that they are. It was the first time that I had shared lunch with someone that I felt I could relate to in years. In his years of life, he has learned how to cope with more problems than I may ever experience. When you develop a mental illness, you will find out who your true friends are. This man said that he has never had much money, but he has always had friends. He also told me that if he had a choice between money and friends, he would take friends. I was almost overwhelmed by this sentiment. I think that he is absolutely right about finding friends. I would not trade my friends for anything.

No matter how hard a family works on recovery, there will be some things that are unavoidable. One problem that I have to face is discrimination. When people find out that a person has a mental illness, it sometimes causes uneasy feelings. Instead of getting angry or feeling sorry for myself, I turn it into positive energy. It is very important for the patient and the family to face discrimination wisely. People are so use to seeing those statistics and horror stories that they forget that they are dealing with a human being. In the early stages of my illness, I had my feelings hurt very seriously. After a while, it is easy to start believing that you cannot achieve the things that healthy people can accomplish. I honestly believe that most people are not trying to discriminate against people with mental illnesses. It is just very easy to stereotype. You and your loved one have got to learn to focus this problem into positive energy. I have found that even after I accomplished several of my long term goals, some people still feel very uneasy around me. I think the most important thing that I learned from discrimination is that you are not going to change people. It is a waste of time to try to change people. It is just important to face your fears and problems with an undying desire. This will bring a feeling that is hard to describe. My hope is, as I face challenges and adversity that someday people will see me as John and that guy with schizophrenia. There were times that I closed my door and cried about the way that I was treated by someone that thought they were better than some guy with mental issues. My advice to the family of the patient and the patient is that everyone has something special to offer the world. I have met a precious few people that have had a lasting impression on my life because they cared about my feelings. People tend to be a little skeptical of things that they do not understand. I use to get angry about the lack of justice for those with mental illnesses. That got me absolutely nowhere. I changed my point of view entirely. Now, I just want to change as many of the problems that are in the system that I can. I encourage the families that face these adversities to do the same. There are organizations that dedicate all their resources to helping those with mental illnesses. I will mention again that I have a resource section at the end of this essay that is dedicated to helping in those times of need. I try to be self-sufficient and face problems head on, but I still ask for help with problems from time to time. My main concern is that families and patients do not let discrimination cause serious problems. Nobody is perfect, but it is important to ask for help if you think that you or a loved one is facing discrimination. What most people do not understand is between the schizophrenia, the medication side effects, and the pressures of life, facing a mental illness is no walk in the park. If everyone could face schizophrenia for one day, I guarantee it would change the way they think about people with this illness.

I have faced some very uneasy times and I have found that some basic things helped me get through. I always called them fun therapy. If your loved one has some pictures that they hold very dear, get together with them and make a photo album or scrap book. With a mental illness, it sometimes feels like comforting days are few and far between. When I put photo albums together, it takes me to brighter days. Some days I sit and look through my wedding photo album a couple of times. Like they say, a picture is worth a thousand words. Flowers also bring a spot of sunshine into the day. When I lived in my apartment, I did not have many friends. I put a flower on the table and made sure it got water. It may sound small, but it brings a positive focus into the room and your life. When I lived in the group home, once a week we would watch a movie that we liked and eat popcorn. It is a good feeling to see people with so many problems having moments of joy. There is something about watching a movie in the dark and eating popcorn that livens up the most terrible mood. Sometimes buying a gift for yourself is comforting. That is why I think that it is important at least once a month to buy something that you really want. I remember buying a compact disc that I really liked and it brought me months of joy. I never was a good cook, but some of my friends in the group home were amazing cooks. I remember seeing them light up when they would try a new recipe. The nice thing about recipes is that you do not have to pay a fortune for them. You can go to the library and get a recipe book. A library card is not very expensive to get, and the libraries always have something fun going on. They have endless resources and they even have computers. I think that a person should read at least one book a year. It is amazing how the imagination can bring subtle emotion when a person reads. With the countless hours that are involved with the recovery process, reading can be a comfort that is hard to replace. I hope it does not sound strange, but something that I found to be relaxing and therapeutic is eating dinner by candle light. There is just something soothing about it.

A mental health patient may sometimes seem irritable. I have already mentioned the pain of medication side effects. It is important to remember that not only is a person that faces a mental illness going through emotional turmoil, but they are facing medication side effects that take some serious getting use to. I would have to say that medication side effects are better than they were a decade ago, but they are still present. When a person with a mental illness seems short, please remember that they are facing these side effects. Sometimes it seems that I cannot get enough sleep. Other times I toss and turn for hours.

I want to spend the rest of this essay talking about people that have been a huge inspiration in my life. There are quite a few people that were so pivotal in my recovery that I feel I must put them in this book.

I want to start my reflection with a great friend of mine, Mark. I cannot stress enough the impact that a person's friends will have on their recovery. If you surround yourself with positive and successful people, odds are you will be positive and successful. I was struggling with an alcohol addiction and I was chain smoking. Mark approached me and he told me that no one is going to change my life. He told me that I would have to change it myself. I have not found any words that had more impact on my life than that. When you find friends that challenge you and are concerned with bettering themselves, you move through a transformation. Mark encouraged me to go back to school. I got a bachelor of science in business administration. This did not put an end to my problems, but it sure did give me more options. I learned that there are grants and scholarships for people with mental illnesses and it can change a person's life. Mark did not have an easy time at every stage of his life, but he still took the time to change my life. One of the things that I picked up from him was determination. If there is a hardship in your life, instead of using it as an excuse to fail, use it as a reason to do even better. I could have given up so many times in my life, but I used those negative situations to drive my determination. When I failed the English and Math placement test, I called Mark. Instead of telling me I should give up on school, he told me to start with entry level classes. I do not think that I have worked on anything else that hard in my entire life. I really enjoyed calling him to say, "Hey, I got an A on my term paper". I spent countless hours working on school projects with him. He never complained about anything we worked on, no matter how many hours it took. That is one friendship that I would not give up for anything in the world. I will spend the rest of my life working to change lives like my friends have done for me.

I would like to continue my reflection with some words about my great grandmother. Thelma Williams is my great grandmother. I cannot count the times that the words of wisdom she gave me as a child have carried over into my adult life. When I was a child, I would watch the seasons change in the scenery that occupied the fields. My great grandparents lived in a small town and I would spend my summers there. My great grandpa had one of his legs amputated and I help take care of him. My great grandmother was very self-sufficient, but she really appreciated the help around the house. I would sit for hours and listen to her talk about how different life was in the times that I did not know. When I was in the recovery process, it was the words of wisdom and comfort that she had given me that made me strong. When I was a child, she told me that there would be hard times and there will be joyous times. She told me that it was the hard time that made a person strong and it was also the hard times that made the joyous times even more enjoyable. I would stay up and ask her to tell me stories about how her life had changed over the years. She worked in a canning factory and my grandpa worked in the tomato fields. She once told me that she had very few regrets. I thought that this was great. This helped me when I went back to school or worked on a very difficult project in life. If I had given up on trying to excel in life when I developed my mental illness, there are some many things that I would have missed out on. I thought that I really do not want to look back on my life and feel regret. I became a nation honor society member in college. I had heard so many times that people with schizophrenia do not do these types of things. I am sure that she was smiling when I got that award. She is always in my heart and that is why I felt her presence when I walked up to get my award. I can remember walking though Nineveh when I was a child. I had no worries in those days and she made sure of that. When I think about her and that town, it is like my worries disappear. It was as if my great grandma was my age. She knew how to make a skinned knee stop hurting and a bad day vanish. She loved her independence. As I mentioned, she appreciated my help, but she wanted to be able to rely on herself. I think that I probably picked up that trait from her. If there were problems, she could always find the bright side. This is a trait that she instilled in my mom. When I have a really bad day, it would be easy to give up. It is like she told me, those bad days make the sweet days even sweeter.

Next, I would like to focus on something that made a lasting difference in my outlook on life. In 2008, I got a black belt in Tae Kwon Do. Most people think that Tae Kwon Do is only about fighting. I did learn a great deal of self-defense, but I also learned a great deal more. I learned what a person can do anthing when they persevere. I have attempted many things in my life and I have not succeeded at everything that I have attempted. I still struggle with self-control, but I recognize this. More than anything, Tae Kwon Do taught me to recognize my weaknesses and learn to strengthen them. I also learned that some people are better at different things than others. By working with others, you can put your strengths together and achieve whatever you want to attempt. Tae Kwon Do taught me to be a good student in both the learning and mentoring portions that are necessary. I really enjoyed working with the students that were in the early stages of the art. Just as I enjoyed learning from those that are in the senior ranks.

I would like to talk about the two people that were there for me in the darkest of my hours. My parents stood with me when I was not sure if I was going to recover. My mother was there almost every day that I was in the hospital. My dad was there almost every day when I had just moved into the group home. What do you say about parents that give up everything that they are doing to make sure a child recovers? I was lost, especially in those first few weeks. My mother was the only reality that I could accept. She would come to the hospital and sit and try to get me to respond to treatment. When I was growing up, I never really saw eye to eye with my mother. After a few weeks of harsh reality, I understood. She really cared about what happened to me. My dad sacrificed so many hours for me when I was living in the group home. I do not think that there is another person that knows and understands me like my dad does. Our family is very strong. I think that a situation like this can either destroy a family or make it stronger. I think it made our lives and relationships stronger. My mother told me that she probably would not have made it through those times without my grandmother. I hope that my family knows that the difference that they have made in my life is appreciated.

I searched in vain for many years before I found someone to share the rest of my life with. On June 20, 2009 I married Kathleen Wills. It is a very special feeling to find someone that loves you and believes in your dreams. Though we have been married only two years, we have experienced some relatively hard times. I still struggle with problems that my mental condition has an adverse effect on. When I walk through the door and see her smile, my pain is gone. After years of ridiculously destructive relationships, finding a person that I love and trust is unimaginably fulfilling. I think that it is hard for a person with a mental illness to find strong relationships. This might be because of the lack of socialization. It might be that it is hard to trust individuals. Or maybe even the fact that mental illnesses are thought to be somewhat taboo. This plagued me for years and I almost let it ruin my life. Kathleen is my constant reminder that you can find happiness in the world. If you or a loved one is struggling emotionally, find strength in your friends and family.

When I was first diagnosed with schizophrenia, I was introduced to Dr. Terry Parrish. I cannot count the times that Dr. Parrish has given lasting advice. Dr. Parrish is an incredible pianist and I admire his love for music. His love for music helped us engage in conversation, even in the early stages of my mental illness. I think that having a common love for something, such as music, can help break barriers. I have a tendency to feel nervous around doctors, but Dr. Parrish and the whole network of staff have made me feel very comfortable. I really think that this comfort and common ground have led to my success. When I was first introduced into the network, I was afraid of failure. It really does help when you are told that you can succeed in life, especially when you admire a person dearly. I wish that I could tell all of those that are in the early stages of a mental illness that it does get better. It takes hope, strength, and guidance to make it through those first few months, but I promise that facing such a problem makes a person very strong. I have also found that honesty is the best policy. If you or a loved one are having problems let your doctor know. I try to be very independent, but a doctor has a very good idea of what can be done to help in times of distress. When I opened the envelope that held my diploma for my bachelor of science, the first thing that I thought was thank you Dr. Parrish.

There are so many people that have changed my life. I would not have made it very far without the compassion of each of these individuals. I am forever grateful and I hope that I can make a difference in the lives of those that are in need.

Resources:

www.nami.org

 www.dare.com

www.lilly.com

 www.astrazeneca.com

www.adultandchild.org

www.ingramcontent.com/pod-product-compliance
Lightning Source LLC
Chambersburg PA
CBHW072139290526
45789CB00013B/1631